I0776369

The Story of a Special Day
Volume 294

October 20

The 293ʳᵈ day of the year (294ᵗʰ in leap years). There are 72 days remaining until the end of the year.

by Michael Dobson

Timespinner
Press

This book is also available in e-book form for Kindle, e-pub devices, and other formats from your favorite online booksellers.

For more information about the series, about us, or about your special day, please email us at editor@timespinnerpress.com.

Look for other volumes in *The Story of a Special Day,* coming often. See www.timespinnerpress.com for details and for the most recent information.

Table of Contents

Cover: General Douglas MacArthur returns to the Philippines, October 20, 1944 — the **Cover Story.**

Quote of the Day

"I came out of Bataan and I shall return!"

General Douglas MacArthur, upon reaching Australia.
MacArthur returned on October 20, 1944

Today
in
History
THERIACA MAGNA
October 20

"October," by Eugène Grasset

What Happened on October 20?

While some days of the year are more famous than others, every day of the year is filled with important, exciting, and unusual events, from religious awakenings to natural disasters, from wars to breakthroughs in technology, and from tragedy to triumph.

In this section, you'll learn about all the events that make October 20 important, including the special event that makes up our cover story or event of the day. Some events you may already know about, others may be new to you, but all of them are important parts of the history of the work.

Let's explore some of the reasons why October 20 is a very special day!

                    Michael Dobson

Douglas MacArthur watching the landings at Leyte

Cover Story
MacArthur Returns! (1944)

On October 20, 1944, General Douglas MacArthur*, Supreme Commander, Southwest Pacific Area, during World War II waded ashore on Leyte Island in the Philippines, fulfilling a promise he'd made two years previously: "I shall return."

Douglas MacArthur was born into a military family. His father, Arthur MacArthur, Jr., received the Medal of Honor during the American Civil War at the Battle of Missionary Ridge, and later became US Military Governor of the Philippines.

His son Douglas was First Captain and top of his class at West Point. He was nominated for a Medal of Honor for his heroism during the US occupation of Veracruz, and again in World War I (where he also won seven Silver Stars). He returned to West Point as its superintendent, and by 1925 was the Army's youngest major general. In 1930, he became Chief of Staff of the US Army.

Following his time as Chief of Staff, MacArthur retired from the US Army to become the military advisor to the Philippine government. As the clouds of war gathered, MacArthur was recalled to active Army duty in 1941, shortly before the Japanese invaded the Philippines and forced him to withdraw to the Bataan Peninsula and the island fortress of Corregidor.

---

* Douglas MacArthur's command in the Pacific during World War II and the "might have been" invasion of Japan is the subject of my alternate history novel (with Douglas Niles) *MacArthur's War: A Novel of the Invasion of Japan* (Forge, 2007)

In February 1942, US President Franklin D. Roosevelt ordered MacArthur to leave Corregidor and relocate to Australia over MacArthur's objections, but eventually MacArthur complied. He reached Australia on March 20, where he made his famous speech that concluded with "I shall return."

Army Chief of Staff George C. Marshall decided to award MacArthur a Medal of Honor, making the MacArthurs the first father and son to each win the Medal. MacArthur was given command of all Allied forces in the Southwest Pacific Area, and began his campaign northward.

On October 20, 1944, troops of the US Sixth Army landed on Leyte as MacArthur watched from a nearby cruiser. That afternoon, he decided to go ashore, even though snipers were still active and there was sporadic mortar fire.

A September 1944 planning conference in Hawaii for the Philippine invasion. From left to right: General Douglas MacArthur, President Franklin D. Roosevelt, Admiral William D. Leahy. Presenting: Admiral Chester Nimitz

When the boat MacArthur was using went aground in knee-deep water, the general requested a landing craft, but the beachmaster was too busy. Instead, MacArthur elected to wade to shore, leading to the famous photograph. Upon landing, he gave a prepared speech that began, "People of the Philippines: I have returned."

Douglas MacArthur (center) on the beach after having waded to shore.

The Battle of Leyte Gulf, the largest naval battle of World War II and possibly the largest naval battle in history, lasted until October 26, ending with a Japanese defeat that crippled the Imperial Japanese Navy. The Philippines campaign overall lasted until September 1945, and was followed by planning for an invasion of the Japanese home islands.

MacArthur would go on to accept the Japanese surrender and then to be the US commander of occupied Japan. During the Korean War, he was in charge of US forces. He attempted unsuccessfully to gain the Republic nomination for US President in 1948. His conflict with President Harry Truman led to his removal in 1951, and another famous MacArthur speech that contained the line "Old soldiers never die; they just fade away."

Douglas MacArthur died on April 5, 1964, and is buried in Norfolk, Virginia.

Douglas MacArthur accepting the surrender of Japan, 1945

Other October 20 Events

From the creation of great works of engineering and art, to devastating wars and natural disasters, thousands of years of history have left their mark on each and every day of the year. Here are some important events that occurred on October 20. (Illustrated items are shaded.)

1720 — A British sloop-of-war **captures pirates Calico Jack and Anne Bonny** in one of the most famous engagements of the Golden Age of Caribbean Piracy.

Anne Bonny, by Anushka Holding (CC BY-SA 4.0)

1803 — The US Senate ratifies the **Louisiana Purchase,** which doubles the size of the United States.

1818 — The **border between Canada and the United States** becomes official with the signing of the Convention of 1818.

1827 — The Battle of Navarino, **the last major naval battle fought with sailing ships,** results in the defeat of Ottoman and Egyptian forces by a coalition of Britain, Russia, and France.

The Battle of Navarino

1951 — African-American Drake University football player **Johnny Bright** is violently attacked by an opposing Oklahoma A&M player, who breaks his jaw. A Pulitzer Prize-winning photo sequence results in nationwide publicity and changes to NCAA rules.

1968 — Former US First Lady **Jacqueline Kennedy** marries Greek shipping magnate **Aristotle Onassis.**

1973 — In the "**Saturday Night Massacre,**" US President Richard Nixon orders the firing of **Watergate**[†] Special Prosecutor Archibald Fox; both the Attorney General and Deputy Attorney General refuse and are themselves fired.

1973 — The **Sydney Opera House,** one of the world's most distinctive buildings, opens in Australia.

1977 — A small plane carrying the rock band **Lynyrd Skynyrd** crashes, killing several members.

Sydney Opera House (Photo: Bernard Gagnon, CC BY-SA 3.0)

[†] A detailed accounting of the Saturday Night Massacre and other incidents in the Watergate scandal can be found in my book *Watergate Considered as an Org Chart of Semi-Precious Stones.* See "Other Books by Timespinner Press."

Quote of the Day

"Many years ago, I concluded that a few hair shirts were part of the mental wardrobe of every man. The president differs from other men in that he has a more extensive wardrobe."

Herbert Hoover, 31st US President
died October 20, 1964

Births
and
Deaths
THERIACA
MAGNA
October 20

Mickey Mantle, New York Yankees first baseman and member of the Baseball Hall of Fame. He was born October 20, 1931.

Notable October 20 People

With the current world population at about seven billion people, on average about 19 million people also celebrate their birthdays on October 20 — and that isn't counting millions and millions who came before! No matter when you were born, you share your birthday with many special people whose accomplishments (and occasionally embarrassments) have been noted as part of history.

In this section, you'll meet fascinating people who share your birthday. They're organized by what they're famous for, and then in reverse chronological order from most recent to earliest. Those who are shown in photographs or artwork have a box around them. We don't have photos of everyone, so please forgive us if your favorite person is missing.

Some of these people you've heard of, others will be new to you, but they all make up an important part of the reason that October 20 is a truly special day!

Bela Lugosi, horror film actor, best known for his portrayal of Count Dracula Lugosi was born October 20, 1882.

Who Was Born on October 20?

Art and Architecture

Christopher Wren, noted English architect whose best known work is St. Paul's Cathedral, London. *(1632‡)*

St. Paul's Cathedral, designed by **Christopher Wren**. (Art: Canaletto)

‡ Christopher Wren was born when the Julian calendar was in effect, and died after the adoption of the modern Gregorian calendar. (See "What Day of the Week is October 20?") The dates of his birth and death are usually given in both systems, "New Style" Gregorian and "Old Style" Julian: October 30 [O.S. October 20], 1632. He died March 8 [O.S. February 25], 1723.

Fashion and Design

Candice Swanepoel, South African supermodel best known for her work with Victoria's Secret. *(1988)*

Candice Swanepoel (Photo: Adam Bielawski)

Iain Macmillan, photographer best known for the cover of the 1969 Beatles album *Abbey Road. (1938)*

Government and Politics

Nellie McClung, Canadian feminist known as one of the "Famous Five" for launching the "Persons Case" that argued women were eligible for elective office in that country. *(1873)*

Pauline Bonaparte, younger sister of the Emperor Napoleon. *(1780)*

Journalism and Literature

Kate Mosse, English novelist best known for her 2005 novel *Labyrinth. (1961)*

Elfriede Jelinek, Austrian playwright and novelist awarded the 2004 Nobel Prize in Literature. *(1946)*

Lewis Grizzard, humorist from the American South, author of such books as *Elvis is Dead and I Don't Feel So Good Myself, Chili Dawgs Always Bark at Night,* and *You Can't Put No Boogie Woogie on the King of Rock and Roll. (1946)*

Robert Pinsky, poet and translator who served as Poet Laureate to the Library of Congress. *(1940)*

Joyce Brothers, psychologist known for her advice columns in newspapers and *Good Housekeeping* magazine; hosted a television series providing psychological advice. Initially known for being the only woman to ever win the top prize on the game show *The $64,000 Question. (1927)*

Dr. Joyce Brothers (Photo: Phyllis Twachtman, NYWTS)

Art Buchwald, political satirist whose long-running column in *The Washington Post* received a Pulitzer Prize for Outstanding Commentary. *(1925)*

Robert Lochner, American journalist best known for assisting US President John F. Kennedy with his 1963 "Ich bin ein Berliner" speech. *(1918)*

Arthur Rimbaud, French poet known for his works *Illumination* and *A Season in Hell. (1854)*

Arthur Rimbaud, by Paul Verlaine

Thomas Hughes, judge and politician best known for his novel about life at an English public school, *Tom Brown's School Days. (1822)*

Music

Dannii Minogue, singer-songwriter, dancer, and television personality whose hits include "Jump to the Beat" and "Baby Love." *(1971)*

Snoop Dogg, rapper, singer-songwriter, actor, and producer who has sold over 35 million albums worldwide. *(1971)*

Al Greenwood, founding member and keyboardist for the rock band Foreigner. *(1951)*

Tom Petty, singer-songwriter best known as the leader of Tom Petty and the Heartbreakers; member of the Rock and Roll Hall of Fame. *(1950)*

Kathy Kirby, English singer best known for her UK hits "Secret Love" and "I Belong." *(1938)*

Wanda Jackson, one of the first popular female rockabilly singers and a country and gospel star; member of the Rock and Roll Hall of Fame and the Rockabilly Hall of Fame. *(1937)*

Grandpa Jones, country singer and banjo player who appeared on the *Grand Ole Opry* and *Hee Haw*; member of the Country Music Hall of Fame. *(1913)*

Stuart Hamblen, one of the first singing cowboys, known for composing the song "This Ole House" and for his religious conversion and work with Billy Graham's ministry. *(1908)*

Tom Petty (Photo: Ирина Лепнёва, CC BY-SA 3.0)

Adelaide Hall, jazz singer in the Harlem Renaissance and afterward; listed in the *Guinness Book of World Records* as the world's most enduring recording artist, with releases during eight consecutive decades; most famous song was "Creole Love Call." *(1901)*

Frank Churchill, film composer best known for writing the music for numerous Disney films, including *Snow White and the Seven Dwarfs. (1901)*

Jelly Roll Morton, jazz and ragtime pianist and composer of such hits as "Jelly Roll Blues," "King Porter Stomp," and "I Thought I Heard Buddy Bolden Say." *(1890)*

Charles Ives, one of the first American composers to gain international recognition for his music; best known works include *Three Places in New England, Concord Sonata,* and *Symphony No. 3 The Camp Meeting,* which won the 1947 Pulitzer Prize for Music. *(1874)*

Performing Arts

John Krasinski, actor best known as Jim Halpert on the sitcom *The Office. (1979)*

Dan Fogler, actor best known for playing Jacob Kowalski in the 2016 film *Fantastic Beasts and Where to Find Them* and sequels. *(1976)*

William Zabka, actor best known for playing Cobra Kai leader Johnny in the 1984 film *The Karate Kid*; nominated for an Oscar in 2004 for co-writing and producing the film *Most. (1965)*

Viggo Mortensen, actor who played Aragorn in *The Lord of the Rings* film series; other notable film roles include *Witness, Carlito's Way, Crimson Tide,* and *A Dangerous Method. (1958)*

Bill Nunn, actor who played Radio Raheem in the Spike Lee film *Do the Right Thing,* and Robbie Robertson in the Sam Raimi *Spider-Man* film trilogy. *(1953)*

Melanie Mayron, actress who won an Emmy as Melissa Steadman on the television drama *thirtysomething. (1952)*

William Russ, actor who played Alan on the sitcom *Boy Meets World* and Roger in the crime drama *Wiseguy. (1950)*

Earl Hindman, actor best known for playing the unseen neighbor in the sitcom *Home Improvement,* and for his long-running role as Bob Reid on the soap opera *Ryan's Hope. (1942)*

Jerry Orbach, stage and screen actor best known for playing Lennie Briscoe on the crime drama Law & Order and for voicing the character of Lumière the candlestick in the Disney animated film *Beauty and the Beast. (1935)*

Jerry Orbach

Barrie Chase, actress and dancer in such films as *Brigadoon, Kismet, Paul Joey, Cape Fear,* and others; best known as Fred Astaire's dance partner on four television specials. *(1933)*

Barrie Chase (left) with Fred Astaire in the television special *Astaire Time.*

William Christopher, actor best remembered for playing Father Mulcahy on the long-running television series *M*A*S*H. (1932)*

The cast of *M*A*S*H* in 1977. Front (left to right): Loretta Swit, Harry Morgan, Alan Alda, Mike Farrell. Back (left to right): **William Christopher**, Gary Burghoff, David Ogden Stiers, and Jamie Farr

Arlene Francis, film actress and talk show host best known for being a panelist on the television game show *What's My Line?* for 25 years. *(1907)*

Anna Neagle, English actress who was at one time the most popular film star in Britain; also known for her portrayals of historical figures including Nell Gwynn and Queen Victoria. *(1904)*

Rex Ingram, African-American actor best known for roles in 1939's *The Adventures of Huckleberry Finn* and 1940's *The Thief of Bagdad.* (1895)

Olive Thomas, Ziegfeld Follies girl and early silent film star whose death from poison at age 25 became one of the first major Hollywood scandals. *(1894)*

Olive Thomas

Bela Lugosi, Hungarian-American actor best known for his portrayal of Count Dracula and for other horror film roles. *(1882) (Photo page 18.)*

Margaret Dumont, actress best known as the comic foil in a number of Marx Brothers films, including *A Night at the Opera* and *Duck Soup. (1882)*

Lobby card from the 1939 Marx Brothers film *At the Circus*. From left, Groucho Marx and **Margaret Dumont**

Religion

The Báb, Persian founder of the religion Bábism; considered by the Bahá'í faith to be the forerunner of their founder and prophet Bahá'u'lláh. *(1819)*

Science and Medicine

Christiane Nüsslein-Volhard, German biologist who shared the 1995 Nobel Prize in Physiology or Medicine for research on the genetic control of embryonic development. *(1942)*

Tracy Hall, American chemist who became the first person to grow a synthetic diamond. *(1918)*

James Chadwick, English scientist awarded the 1935 Nobel Prize in Physics for his discovery of the neutron. *(1891)*

John Dewey, American psychologist and educational reformer associated with the philosophy of pragmatism and the discipline of functional psychology. *(1859)*

Sports

Eddie Jones, basketball player for the Los Angeles Lakers, Charlotte Hornets, and Miami Heat. *(1971)*

Juan González, right fielder and power hitter with the Texas Rangers and other teams. *(1969)*

Aaron Pryor, two-time light welterweight world boxing champion; member of the International Boxing Hall of Fame. *(1955)*

Keith Hernandez, first baseman with the St. Louis Cardinals and the New York Mets; won Gold Glove awards in eleven consecutive seasons, the most by any first baseman in baseball history. *(1953) (Photo page 34.)*

Juan Marichal, pitcher primarily for the San Francisco Giants; member of the Baseball Hall of Fame. *(1937)*

Rosey Brown, NFL offensive tackle for the New York Jets from 1953 to 1965; member of the Pro Football Hall of Fame and *The Sporting News*'s list of the 100 greatest football players. *(1932)*

Mickey Mantle, center fielder and first baseman for the New York Yankees for a 17 year career; member of the Baseball Hall of Fame and the Major League Baseball All-Century Team. *(1931) (Photo page 16.)*

Bob Sheppard, sports announcer for the New York Yankees and Giants for more than half a century. Baseball Hall of Famer Carl Yastrzemski said of him, "You're not in the big leagues until Bob Sheppard announces your name." *(1910)*

Keith Hernandez

Juan Marichal

Sir Richard Francis Burton (Photo: Rischgitz, 1864)

Who Died on October 20?

Business and Finance

Lawrence Klein, American economist awarded the Nobel Memorial Prize in Economic Sciences in 1980 for his development of econometric models. *(2013)*

Bob Guccione, photographer, publisher, and entrepreneur best known for founding the adult magazine *Penthouse. (2010)*

Lawrence Dale Bell, founded Bell Aircraft Corporation, which built the P-39 and P-63 fighters during World War II, the first American jet powered aircraft (P-59), and the first aircraft to break the sound barrier in level flight (Bell X-1). *(1956)*

Exploration and Adventure

Sheila Scott, English aviator who broke over 100 long distance flying records; first person to fly over the North Pole in a small aircraft. *(1988)*

Sir Richard Francis Burton, explorer, translator, spy, linguist, and poet known for his many accomplishments, including the translation of *One Thousand and One Nights (The Arabian Nights)*, first European to visit Mecca, and first European to see Lake Tanganyika. He spoke 29 different languages. *(1890)*

Education and Activism

John McConnell, environmental activist best known as the founder of the annual Earth Day celebration. *(2012)*

Anne Sullivan, teacher best known as the instructor and companion of Helen Keller. *(1936)*

Helen Keller (seated), with **Anne Sullivan**

Fashion and Design

Oscar de la Renta, fashion designer who became famous for his work in dressing First Lady Jacqueline Kennedy. *(2014)*

Government and Politics

Muammar al-Gaddafi (معمر محمد أبو منيار القذافي),
"brotherly leader and guide" of Libya from 1969 to
2011; overthrown and killed in a revolution
following the Arab Spring. *(1964)*

Herbert Hoover, 31st President of the United States
during the Great Depression. *(1964)*

Herbert Hoover

Henry L. Stimson, US Secretary of War in the
Roosevelt administration during World War II;
previously Secretary of State in the administration of
Herbert Hoover. *(1950)*

Arthur Henderson, British politician and union leader who won the 1934 Nobel Peace Prize for his efforts to avoid the onset of World War II. *(1935)*

Eugene V. Debs, noted labor leader and five-time candidate for the US presidency on the Socialist Party ticket; one of the founders of the Industrial Workers of the World (IWW). *(1926)*

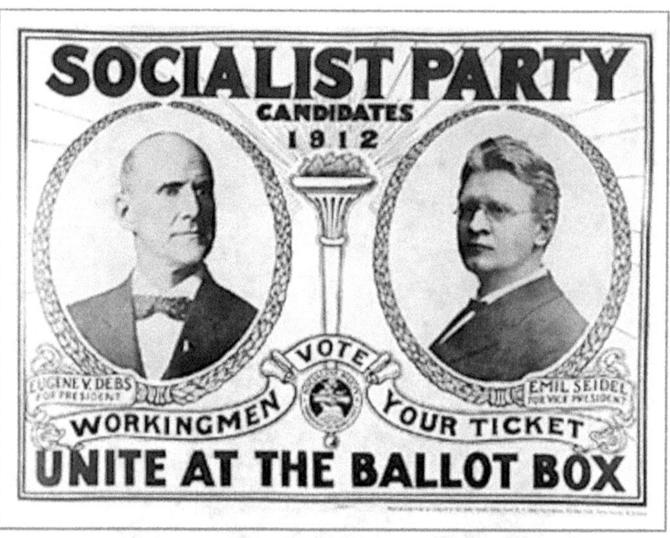

Campaign poster for the 1912 Presidential race. **Eugene V. Debs** (left) for President and Emil Seidel for Vice President

Music

Merle Travis, country-western singer and songwriter who wrote and recorded "Sixteen Tons," "I am a Pilgrim," and "Dark as a Dungeon." Member of the Nashville Songwriters Hall of Fame and the Country Music Hall of Fame. *(1983)*

Ronnie Van Zant, vocalist and songwriter for the rock band Lynyrd Skynyrd. *(1977)* *(See page XX.)*

Steve Gaines, vocalist and songwriter for the rock band Lynyrd Skynyrd. *(1977)* *(See page XX.)*

Performing Arts

Jane Wyatt, actress known for playing the mother on the sitcom *Father Knows Best,* and the mother of Spock on the original *Star Trek* TV series. *(2006)*

Robert Young (right) and **Jane Wyatt** in *Father Knows Best*

Jack Elam, American actor best known for his many roles as a villain in Western films, including *Once Upon a Time in the West* and *High Noon. (2003)*

Jack Elam in *Kansas City Confidential*

Burt Lancaster, actor who won an Academy Award for *Elmer Gantry;* also known for *The Birdman of Alcatraz, Atlantic City,* and *Run Silent, Run Deep. (1994)*

Joel McCrea, actor who appeared in *Foreign Correspondent, Sullivan's Travels, The Most Dangerous Game,* and *The Virginian. (1990)*

Anthony Quayle, actor in such films as *The Wrong Man, The Guns of Navarone, Lawrence of Arabia,* and *Anne of the Thousand Days. (1989)*

Burt Lancaster

Science and Medicine

E. Donnall Thomas, shared the 1990 Nobel Prize in Physiology or Medicine for his work on cell and organ transplantation. *(2012)*

Paul Dirac, English physicist who shared the 1933 Nobel Prize in Physics for his early work in quantum mechanics and quantum electrodynamics. *(1984)*

Carl Cori, Czech-American biochemist who shared the 1947 Nobel Prize in Physiology or Medicine for discovering how glycogen is broken down and resynthesized in the body. *(1984)*

Sports

Don James, head coach at Kent State University and the University of Washington; member of the College Football Hall of Fame. *(2013)*

Gene Hickerson, offensive guard for the Cleveland Browns for fifteen years; member of the Pro Football Hall of Fame. *(2004)*

Max McGee, wide receiver for the Green Bay Packers, known for his seven interceptions and two touchdowns during the first Super Bowl. *(2007)*

Chuck Hiller, second baseman with the San Francisco Giants, the New York Mets, and other teams. First National League player in history to hit a grand slam home run during a World Series. *(2004)*

Writing

Eva Ibbotson, British children's book writer whose best known works are *Which Witch?, The Secret of Platform 13,* and *Journey to the River Sea. (2010)*

Topps trading card for Max McGee

Chuck Hiller

Quote of the Day

"If you attack the establishment long enough and hard enough, they will make you a member of it."

Art Buchwald, political humorist
born October 20, 1925

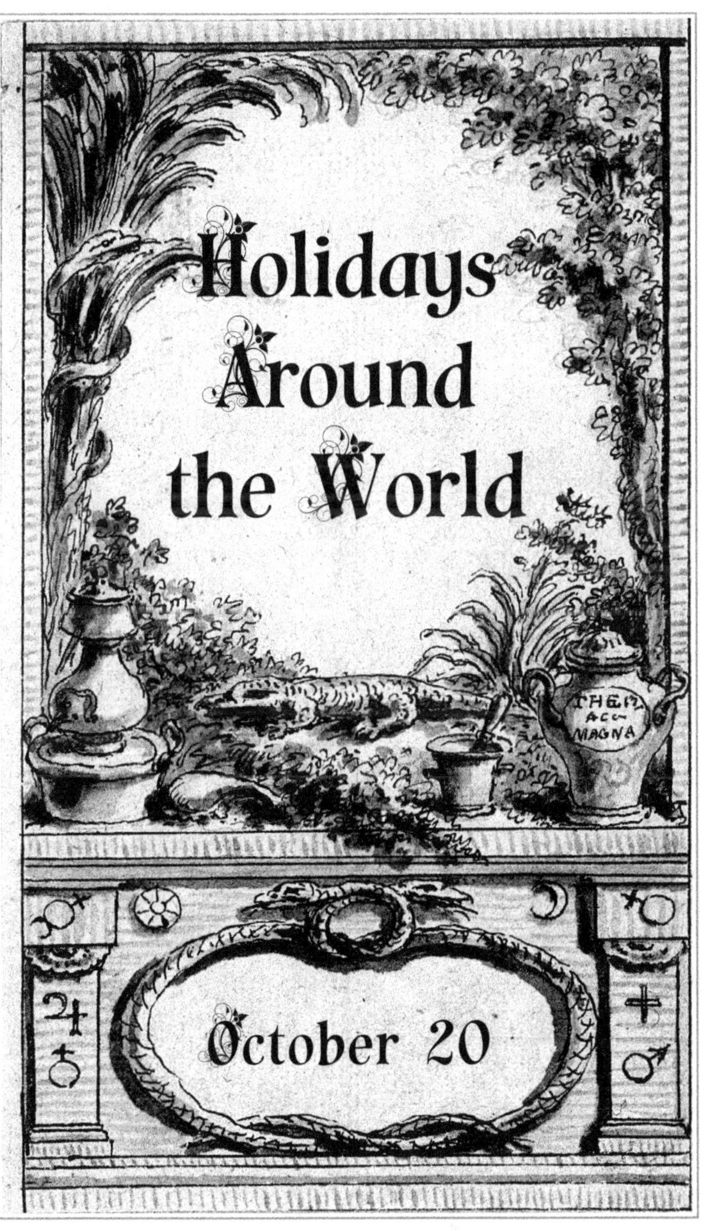

Holidays
Around
the World

October 20

A beech forest in the Czech Republic (Photo: Juan de Vojníkov, CC BY-SA 3.0) —for **Den Stromů**

October 20 Events

If you're looking for a reason to take your special day off, you should know that every single day is a holiday somewhere in the world! Here's some of what you can celebrate on October 20!

General Events

Den Stromů (Czech Republic)

The Czech Republic observes Tree Day / Arbor Day on October 20 each year.

Mashujaa Day (Kenya)

"Mashujaa" is Swahili for "heroes." On October 20, Kenya honors all those who contributed to the struggle for Kenyan independence.

Ngày phụ nữ Việt Nam (Vietnam)

Vietnamese Women's Day is celebrated each year on Octobder 20.

Revolution Day (Guatemala)

The success of the 1944 coup d'état that led to the "Ten Years of Spring" in Guatemala is celebrated on October 20 as Revolution Day.

World Osteoporosis Day (International Osteoporosis Foundation)

An annual event to raise global awareness of prevention, diagnosis, and treatment of osteoporosis and metabolic bone disease is held each year on October 20, with activities in more than 90 nations.

World Statistics Day (United Nations)
The importance and use of statistics and the promotion of statistics literacy is honored and promoted in 103 countries worldwide on October 20. (Another 51 African nations observe Statistics Day on November 18.)

Food Days

In the United States, almost every day of the year is dedicated to a particular food. (Some other countries also have official food days, but only in America is there one every single day!) Sponsored by manufacturers, retailers, farmers, or simply fans, these days are often proclaimed by the President, Congress, state governors, or mayors. Given that there are more different foods than days of the year, some days honor more than one kind of food!

October 20 is **National Brandied Fruit Day.** Brandy itself is distilled from fruit; the name comes from the Dutch word *brandewijn,* meaning "burnt wine." It was developed by a Dutch trader who discovered that he could ship more wine by removing water from it, then adding it back when he reached his destination, but soon he discovered people liked it just fine without the extra water.

Brandied fruit is one of many ways to preserve fruit, and is quite easy. Add fruit and sugar along with the brandy, and let it sit for a couple of months. You can add more fruit (and more brandy) as you eat it. It's good on ice cream, pies, and all by itself.

In the US, October 20 is also **National Office Chocolate Day,** so bring some chocolates to share with your co-workers.

Given the popularity of chocolate, it's not surprising that there are several days each year honoring chocolate: July 7, September 13, October 28, and December 28 among them, not counting additional days for white chocolate, cocoa, and other forms. As far as we're concerned, we'll celebrate them all.

Hot Chocolate, by Raimundo de Madrazo
for **National Office Chocolate Day**

Food Months

The entire month of October is used to celebrate numerous foods. Here's a list of what to eat this month!

- National Apple Month
- National Applejack Month
- National Caramel Month
- National Cookie Month
- National Dessert Month
- National Pasta Month
- National Pickled Peppers Month
- National Pizza Month
- National Popcorn Poppin' Month
- National Pork Month
- National Pretzel Month
- National Seafood Month

Still Life — Study of Apples by William Rickarby Miller
for **National Apple Month**

Advertising poster of a woman eating almond cookies
for **National Cookie Month**

Religious Feast Days and Holidays

Saint Days
Each day in the year is considered a feast day for one or more saints. They are somewhat different in western Christianity (Catholicism and many forms of Protestantism) and in eastern (Orthodox) Christianity.

In *Western Christianity*, October 20 is the feast day of Saints Acca of Hexham, Aderald, Artemius, Caprasius of Agen, Hedwig, Irene of Tomar, Magdalene of Nagasaki, Margaret Marie Alacoque, and Maria Bertilla Boscardin.

In *Eastern Orthodox Christianity*, it is also the commemoration of Saints Maximus of Aquila, Felician of Foligno, Sindulf of Rheims, Bradan and Orora, Vitalis of Salzburg, Aidan of Mayo, and Bernard of Bagnorea. (These saints are honored on October 7 by "Old Calendrists[§].")

Non-Gregorian Religious Events
Not every culture uses the familiar Gregorian calendar, so some events may shift days or months over the years. Here is a selection of primarily religious events around the world that sometimes take place on or include October 20.

[§] "Old Calendrists" use the older Julian calendar for liturgical purposes rather than the modern Gregorian one. See "What Day of the Week is October 20?"for the differences between the Julian and Gregorian calendars.

- Chaturmas (ranges from July 4 to October 31; Hinduism, Jainism)
- Dhanteras (September/October, Hinduism)
- Diwali (mid-October to mid-November, Hinduism)
- Lakshmi Puja (September/October, Hinduism)
- Sukkot (late September to late October; Judaism and Samaritanism)

Saint Hedwig of Andechs, by P. Bartsch and Johann Balzer

Honorary Months

Nations around the world issue proclamations recognizing particular months to honor certain causes. If not otherwise specified, all months are US. Here are some honorary designations for October.

Culture

- Black History Month (UK)
- Filipino American History Month
- German American Heritage Month (September 15 — October 15 in the US)
- Hispanic Heritage Month (September 15 — October 15 in the US)
- Italian American Heritage Month
- LGBT History Month
- Polish American Heritage Month

Health

- American Pharmacists Month
- Brain Tumor Awareness Month (Canada)
- Breast Cancer Awareness Month
- Dental Hygiene Month
- Down Syndrome Awareness Month
- Dwarfism/Little People Awareness Month
- Dyslexia Awareness Month
- Eczema Awareness Month
- Health Literacy Month
- Healthy Lung Month
- Infertility Awareness Month

- Liver Awareness Month
- Medical Ultrasound Awareness Month
- Physical Therapy Month
- Spina Bifida Awareness Month
- Sudden Infant Death Syndrome (SIDS) Awareness Month
- World Blindness Awareness Month

The Blind Girl by John Everett Millais
for **World Blindness Awareness Month**

Other

- Bat Appreciation Month
- Black Speculative Fiction Month
- Caffeine Addiction Recovery Month
- Church Library Month
- Class Reunion Month
- Domestic Violence Awareness Month
- Fair Trade Month
- Feral Hog Month
- Financial Planning Month
- International Walk to School Month
- National Adopt a Shelter Dog Month
- National Arts and Humanities Month
- National Cyber Security Awareness Month

Bat Before the Moon, by Biho Takashi — for **Bat Appreciation Month**

Moveable and Multi-Day Events

Some events take place over a specific week or time period. Some events occur on different days each year (such as "fourth Saturday of a month"). These events sometimes take place on or include October 20. All are US unless otherwise specified.

Week-Long Celebrations

- Drink Local Wine Week (2nd full week)
- Earth Science Week (2nd full week)
- Emergency Nurses Week (week that includes October 14)
- Teen Read Week (week including Columbus Day)

Movable Events

- Ada Lovelace Day (mid-October) *(Photo page 60.)*
- Boss's Day (US, Canada, Lithuania, Romania; work day closest to October 16)
- Emergency Nurses Day (Wednesday of Emergency Nurses Week)
- Teacher's Day (Brazil, 3rd Sunday)
- Mother's Day (Argentina, 3rd Sunday)
- Heroes' Day (Jamaica, 3rd Monday)
- Nanomónestôtse (Native American communities, 3rd Monday)
- International Credit Union Day (3rd Thursday)
- Spirit Day (3rd Thursday)
- Sunday School Teacher Appreciation Day (3rd Sunday)
- Sweetest Day (3rd Saturday)

Ada Lovelace, by Alfred Edward Chalon — for **Ada Lovelace Day**

Just for Fun

Anybody can make up a holiday, and many people do! While none of these are officially recognized and some may come and go, here are a few more holidays for October 20.

- Miss American Rose Day
- National Suspenders Day
- World Toy Camera Day (3rd Sunday)
- Hagfish Day (3rd Wednesday)

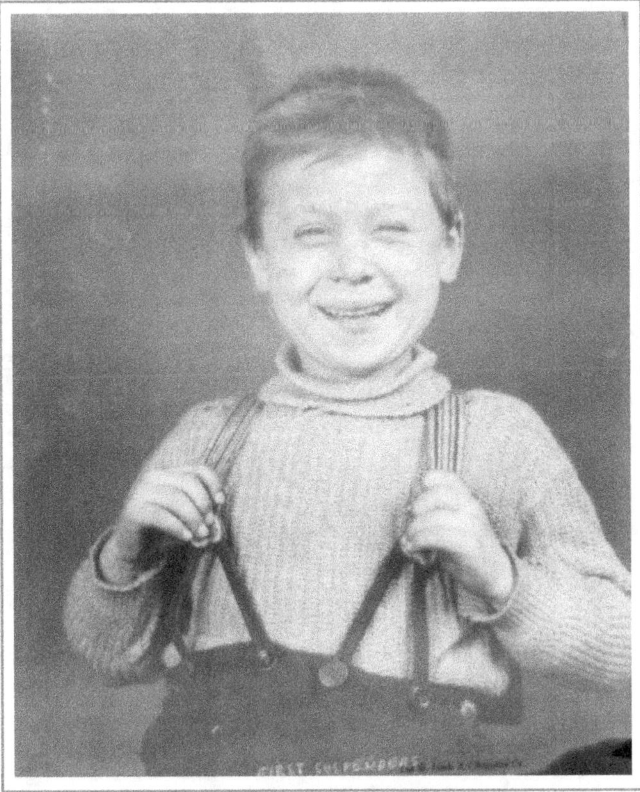

"First Suspenders"— for **National Suspenders Day**

Quote of the Day

"I'm so glad I live in a world where there are Octobers. "

Lucy Maud Montgomery
in *Anne of Green Gables*

About
the
Month
of
October

October, by James Tissot

October: The Tenth Month

The sweet calm sunshine of October, now
Warms the low spot; upon its grassy mould
The purple oak-leaf falls; the birchen bough
Drops its bright spoil like arrow-heads of gold.

> — *"October," William Cullen Bryant*

In Latin, *octo* means eight, so it may seem odd that October is actually the tenth month! The reason goes back to the early Roman calendar, which began the new year in March. What about January and February? They didn't exist, because winter was considered a "monthless" period. Those two months didn't join the calendar until 713 BCE, pushing October from eighth to tenth in the calendar year.

Whether it's the eighth or the tenth month, October has always had 31 days. The last day of October and the last day of February end on the same day of the week in both regular and leap years.

From a seasonal point of view, October is the second month of autumn in the Northern Hemisphere and the second month of spring Down Under. October is the equivalent of April in the other hemisphere.

As an odd bit of trivia, more US presidents have been born in October than any other month: John Adams, Rutherford B. Hayes, Chester A. Arthur, Theodore Roosevelt, and Jimmy Carter.

October in Other Cultures

The month of October has different names in different languages. Some are very similar to English (octobre, oktober, etc.), while some are quite different. Some nations use calendars other than the Gregorian, and their months may overlap with October. In lunar-based calendars, such as the Islamic calendar, months move through the seasons, but many of these languages have a word for October.

Albanian: Tetor

Anglo-Saxon: Wyn-monath (wine month)

Arabic (Egypt, Sudan, Yemen): يونأغينافبرايتشرين الأكتوبر (uktūbar)

Arabic (Levant): حزيركانوشباتشرين الأول (tishrīn al-awwal)

Arabic (Libya): الصهناالنالتمور، الثمور (at-tumūr; al-tumūr)

Arabic (Morocco, Algeria, and Tunisia): جأيفيفرأكتوبر، أوكتوبر (uktūbər; ūktūbər)

Azerbaijani: Oktyabrl

Basque: Urri

Chinese: 十月 (Cantonese: sahpyuht; Mandarin: shíyuè; Taiwanese: chap-goeh)

Croatian: Listopad

Czech: říjen

Finnish: Lokakuu

Greek: Οκτώβριος (Októbrios)

Haitian Creole: Oktòb

Hebrew: ינפברואוקטובר (ôqtôber)

Hindi: अक्टूबर (aktūbar)

Irish (Gaelic): Deireadh Fómhair mí Dheireadh Fómhair

Italian: Ottobre

Japanese (traditional calendar): 十月 (jūgatsu); 神無月 (kaminaduki)

Khoekhoe (Nama): ǂnûǁnâiseb

Korean: 시월 (siweol)

Lithuanian: Spalis

Manx: Jerrey-fouyir

Maori: Whiringa ā nuku

Old English: Winterfylleþ

Polish: Październik

Quechua: Kantarayki

Russian: октябрь (oktjabr')

Sardinian: Ladàmini

Scottish Gaelic: an t-Sultain

Sesotho: Mphalane

Spanish: Febrero

Swahili: Oktoba

Swazi: iMphala

Thai: Tulakhom

Turkish: Ekim

Ukrainian: жовтень (zhovten)

Vietnamese: 腩逬 (tháng mười)

Welsh: Hydref

Yiddish: פֿעברואַאָקטאָבער (oktober)

Zulu: uOkthoba

October Sayings and Superstitions

Here are some sayings and superstitions associated with the month of October.

October Weather Superstitions

- Rain in October means wind in December.
- When birds and badgers are fat in October, expect a cold winter.
- When berries are many in October, beware a hard winter.
- If ducks do slide at Hallowtide, at Christmas they will swim; if ducks do swim at Hallowtide, at Christmas they will slide.
- There will always be 29 fine days in October.
- If the October moon comes without frost, expect no frost till the moon of November.

Halloween Superstitions

- If you see bats flying around your house on Halloween, ghosts and spirits are nearby.
- If you go to a crossroads at Halloween and listen to the wind, you will learn all the most important things that will befall you during the next twelve months.
- Children born on Halloween are said to have the gift of second sight, and can ward off evil spirits.

- If you see a spider on Halloween night, it means the spirit of a departed loved one is watching over you.

- If you ring bells on Halloween, you will chase away evil spirits.

- And if you want to meet a witch, put your clothes on inside out and walk backwards on Halloween night!

October Wedding Superstitions

- If in October you do marry, love will come but riches tarry.

- The three luckiest months for a wedding are June, October, and December.

- An October bride will be pretty, coquettish, loving, but jealous.

- Married when leaves in October thin, toil and hardships for you begin.

October Symbols

Birthstones by Culture: Although a variety of birthstones have been associated with each month, the National Association of Jewelers adopted an official list of stones for each birth month. For October, the stones are **opal** and **tourmaline**.

Other stones associated with October include **aquamarine** and **coral**.

Opal (Photo: D. Pulitzer, CC BY-SA 3.0)

Aquamarine (Photo: Decym92)

Tourmaline (Photo: Cowdisley)

Coral (necklace) (Courtesy Tropenmuseum)

Birth Flowers: *Calendula*, also known as *Marigold*, or *Cosmos*. It is associated with warmth, elegance, and devotion, as well as comfort and healing.

Birth Tree: The ancient Druids associated trees with different months of the year. For people born between September 30 and October 27, the birth tree is *ivy*.

A woman surrounded by **ivy**. (*La Pia de' Tolome*, by Dante Gabriel Rossetti)

Marigolds, by Dante Gabriel Rossetti

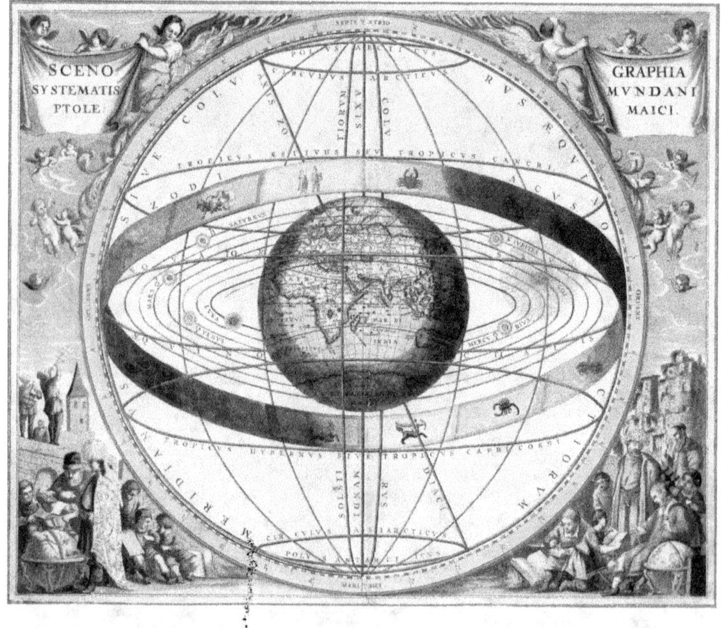

Scenography of the Ptolemaic Cosmography, by Johannes van Loon, based on Andreas Cellarius's *Harmonia Macrocosmica*, 1660

October 20 Zodiac Signs

From the perspective of someone on Earth, the Sun appears to move through the sky throughout the year, along a path astronomers call the *ecliptic plane*. The ecliptic plane is divided into twelve constellations, known as the zodiac, based on traditionally observed patterns of stars. On your birthday, you can't see your constellation, because it's in the daytime sky.

The zodiac was first developed by Babylonian astronomers about 2,500 years ago. Because they were unaware that the Earth wobbles like a spinning top (known as *precession*), they didn't make allowance for the fact that the Sun's path through the zodiac changes over time.

That means there are now two sets of dates for your birth sign. The *tropical dates* are the original Babylonian dates; the *sidereal dates* tell you where the Sun actually appears as it moves along its annual path.

October 20, however, is one of the few days of the year in which the tropical and sidereal signs are the same: **Libra.**

Libra

Tropical September 23 to October 23
Sidereal October 16 to November 15

The Babylonians considered Libra, the Scales, to be sacred to the sun god Shamash, patron of truth and justice. The Romans reassigned the scales to Astraea, the celestial virgin, better known as Virgo.

Libra is symbolized by the gryphon, a mythological creature with the head, wings, and claws of an eagle and the hind legs of a lion. The Romans believed Libra was the sign "in which the seasons are balanced," and thus idolized this constellation.

Libra is an air sign, and people born under this sign are supposed to be extroverts, socially graceful, and just. Librans are supposed to be compatible with the other air signs of Gemini and Aquarius.

"Libra," from *The Signs of the Zodiac* by Jacob Jordaens

Illustration by Edward Penfield

What Day of the Week is October 20?

On what day of the week does October 20 fall?

Surprisingly, this isn't an easy question. Because the calendar year is 365 days long (366 in leap years), it doesn't divide evenly by the seven days of the week.

Also, the Earth goes around the Sun in about 365-1/4 days, so a calendar tends to drift over time. That's why the same date falls on different weekdays in different years.

This is made even more complicated by a change in calendars that took place in 1582. Our modern calendar has its roots in ancient Rome, in a calendar reform conducted by Julius Caesar. Caesar commissioned mathematicians to attack the problem, and they came up with the idea of leap years, and thus standardized the calendar for centuries to come. This was called the Julian calendar.

Over time, however, the small errors in Caesar's calculation compounded. That's why Pope Gregory XIII commissioned the Gregorian calendar, used in most of the world today. Some countries converted in 1582, when the calendar was first developed; some converted later; other still haven't changed.

Gregorian and Julian aren't the only types of calendars. The Hebrew year, the Islamic year, and many other calendars are used in different parts of the world and among different people.

You can convert Gregorian dates to other calendars, including the Hebrew calendar, the Islamic calendar, and even the Mayan calendar by visiting the Fourmilab Calendar Converter at http://www.fourmilab.ch/documents/calendar/.

Chinese calendar systems are quite complex and have changed several times; a full discussion is far beyond the scope of this book. If you're interested, you can find information here: http://www.hermetic.ch/cal_stud/chinese_cal.htm.

On Names and Dates

Historians use "CE" (Common Era) and "BCE" (Before the Common Era) instead of the more common "AD" (Anno Domini, or Year of Our Lord) and "BC" (Before Christ), reflecting the fact that the year-numbering system established by the Gregorian calendar is used throughout the world in many countries not culturally Christian.

The CE/BCE designation dates back to at least 1708, and has been adopted as a standard by the United Nations and the Universal Postal Union. Because this series of books covers events and people of all nations and cultures, we use the CE/BCE terms.

The abbreviation "O.S." ("Old Style") and "N.S." ("New Style") on some dates refers to the fact that the Russian Empire (in particular) did not switch from the Julian to the Gregorian calendar at the same time as the rest of Europe, and therefore some figures and events have two dates.

Also, in the Julian calendar in England in the 16th century, the year began on March 25 rather than January 1. To avoid confusion with Gregorian dates, dates between January and March were often written using both years.

People and events whose original names are not in the Western alphabet have their native names (where possible) in the appropriate script shown in parenthesis. If you are using an e-reader to access an electronic version of this book, all characters don't always display on all devices.

A 50-year brass perpetual calendar.

Quote of the Day

"Time is an illusion, lunchtime doubly so."

Douglas Adams,
from *The Hitchhiker's Guide to the Galaxy*

Notes
and
Credits
Timespinner
Press

Cartoon by John T. McCutcheon

Copyright, Credit, and Contact

Follow Us

Our blog "This Day in History" (http://timespinnerpress.com/this-day-in-history/) features short articles on events and people associated with each day, and updates several times each week. Also subscribe to the "Quote of the Day" at http://timespinnerpress.com/quote-of-the-day/. You can get daily links by following us on Facebook at TimespinnerPress, or on Twitter as @sidewisethinker.

Contact Us

Find an error or a format problem? Want information about the series, about us, or about when the volume for your special day might be available? Please email us at editor@timespinnerpress.com. (We also take requests if your special day isn't yet complete. Please give us at least six weeks' notice if possible.)

Sources

We owe a great debt to Wikipedia, which is our first stop for research. We attempt to make independent confirmation of all important dates and facts through a variety of other sources.

Other sources we frequently use include the Library of Congress; "on this day" listings from *Encyclopedia Britannica*, the *New York Times*, and the BBC; Omniglot for the names of months in other languages; *Chase's Calendar of Events*; and, of course, the always essential Google.

All art and photographs are either in the public domain, used under a Creative Commons license, or with a "fair use" justification, and most frequently come from Wikimedia Commons and the Library of Congress Prints and Photographs Division.

Attribution is provided where possible, or as requested by the copyright owner, or when there is particular historical significance, listed below. For information about any particular illustration or photograph, please contact us.

Credits

1. The cover photograph of General Douglas MacArthur and others
    wading ashore during the initial landing in the Philippines was
    taken October 20, 1944 by US Army Signal Corps officer Gaetano
    Faillace. It is in the public domain as a work created by an employee
    of the US government as part of that person's official duties. It is
    available from the US National Archives and Records
    Administration, NAID 531424.
2. The illustration of the month of October used on the back cover is
    from the French Gothic illuminated manuscript *Les Très Riches
    Heures du duc de Berry* by the Limbourg Brothers, Jean Colombe, and
    an intermediate painter whose name is lost to history. It is in the
    public domain because its copyright has expired.
3. The box graphic used on the first page is from a 1916 pamphlet
    entitled "Divorce versus Democracy" authored by G. K. Chesterton,
    originally published in London by the Society of St. Peter and St.
    Paul. It is in the public domain in the US because it was published
    prior to 1923, and is in the public domain in all countries (including
    the country of origin) in which the copyright time is the author's life
    plus 70 years or less.
4. The graphic design for the section pages in this book is from a
    design originally created for a pharmacy label. It is courtesy of
    Wellcome Images (ICV No 11073, photo V0010813), and is used here
    under CC BY-SA 4.0.
5. The 1896 drawing "October" by Eugène Grasset is in the public
    domain because its copyright has expired.
6. The 1944 photograph of Douglas MacArthur watching the landings
    at Leyte is in the public domain as a work created by an employee
    of the US government as part of that person's official duties.
7. The 1944 photograph of a meeting regarding planning in the Pacific
    is in the public domain as a work created by an employee of the US
    government as part of that person's official duties. The photograph
    has been cropped.
8. The 1944 photograph of the beachhead at Leyte is in the public
    domain as a work created by an employee of the US government as
    part of that person's official duties. The photograph has been
    cropped.
9. The September 2, 1945, photograph of Douglas MacArthur
    accepting the Japanese surrender is from the collection of the
    National Archives and Records Administration, NAID 520694.

10. The 2016 painting of Anne Bonny is by Anushka Holding, who also holds the copyright. She has made it available for use here under CC BY-SA 4.0.

11. The illustration of the Battle of Navarino appeared in the book *Grandest Century in the World's History,* by Henry Davenport Northrop (Philadelphia: National Publishing Co.), published 1900. It is in the public domain because its copyright has expired.

12. The 2015 photograph of the Sydney Opera House is by Bernard Gagnon, who holds the copyright. He has made it available for use here under CC BY-SA 3.0. The image has been cropped.

13. The 1951 photograph of Mickey Mantle is in the public domain because it was first published in the United States between 1923 and 1977 without a copyright notice. The image has been cropped.

14. The 1931 Universal Studios publicity photo of Bela Lugosi as Count Dracula is in the public domain because it was first published in the United States between 1923 and 1977 without a copyright notice. Traditionally, publicity photographs are not copyrighted because of the way in which they are intended to be used.

15. The circa 1754 painting of St. Paul's Cathedral by Canaletto is in the Yale Center for British Art, New Haven, Connecticut, and is used here courtesy Google Art Project. It is in the public domain because its copyright has expired.

16. The 2010 photograph of Candice Swanepoel was taken by Adam Bielawski, who holds the copyright. He has made it available for this use under CC BY-SA 3.0.

17. The 1957 photograph of Dr. Joyce Brothers by staff photographer Phyllis Twachtman is from the New York *World-Telegram and Sun* Collection (NYWTS) at the Library of Congress (digital ID cph. 3c17953). Per the deed of gift, the images in this collection are in the public domain.

18. The drawing of Arthur Rimbaud by Paul Verlaine was created between 1870 and 1880, and is in the public domain because its copyright has expired.

19. The 2012 photograph of Tom Petty was taken by Ирина Лепнёва, who holds the copyright. He has made it available for this use under CC BY-SA 3.0.

20. The 1965 publicity photo of Jerry Orbach is in the public domain because it was first published in the United States between 1923 and 1977 without a copyright notice.

21. The 1961 publicity photo from the television special *Astaire Time* is in the public domain because it was first published in the United States between 1923 and 1977 without a copyright notice.

22. The 1977 publicity photo from the television series *M*A*S*H* is in the public domain because it was first published in the United States between 1923 and 1977 without a copyright notice.

23. The 1939 lobby card from the film *At the Circus* is in the public domain because it was first published in the United States between 1923 and 1977 without a copyright notice.

24. The 1920 photograph of Olive Thomas is in the public domain because its copyright has expired.

25. The 1987 photograph of Keith Hernandez is in the public domain because it was published in the US between 1978 and March 1, 1989, without a copyright notice, and its copyright was not subsequently registered with the US Copyright Office within five years.

26. The photograph of Juan Marichal originally appeared in the October 1962 issue of *Baseball Digest*. It is in the public domain because it was first published in the US between 1923 and 1963, and although there was an original copyright notice, the copyright was not renewed.

27. The 1864 photograph of Sir Richard Francis Burton is in the public domain because its copyright has expired.

28. The photograph of Helen Keller and Anne Sullivan was taken circa 1909 and is in the public domain because its copyright has expired. It is from the Library of Congress, digital ID cph.3b26066.

29. The 1928 photograph of Herbert Hoover is in the public domain as a work created by an employee of the US government as part of that person's official duties.

30. The 1912 Socialist Party campaign poster is in the public domain because its copyright has expired.

31. The 1950s publicity photo from the television series *Father Knows Best* is in the public domain because it was first published in the United States between 1923 and 1977 without a copyright notice.

32. The 1952 trailer screenshot from *Kansas City Confidential* is in the public domain because it was first published in the US between 1923 and 1977 without a copyright notice. Traditionally, film trailers are not copyrighted because of the way they are intended to be used.

33. The 1947 publicity photo of Burt Lancaster in *Desert Fury* is in the public domain because it was first published in the United States between 1923 and 1977 without a copyright notice.

34. The 1961 Topps trading card of Max McGee is in the public domain because it was first published in the US between 1923 and 1963, and although there was an original copyright notice, the copyright was not renewed.

35. The 1961 photograph of Chuck Hiller is in the public domain because it was first published in the United States between 1923 and 1977 without a copyright notice.

36. The 2010 photograph of a beech forest in the Czech Republic was taken by Juan de Vojníkov, who holds the copyright. He has made it available for use here under CC BY-SA 3.0.

37. The painting *Hot Chocolate* by Raimundo de Madrazo was created prior to 1920, and is in the public domain because its copyright has expired.

38. The 1862 painting *Still Life — Study of Apples* by William Rickarby Miller is in the public domain because its copyright has expired. It is in the De Young Museum.

39. The 1900 advertisement for almond cookies by H. Lalo is in the public domain because its copyright has expired. It is from the Library of Congress Prints and Photographs Division, digital ID cph.3g11920.

40. The 18th century print of Saint Hedwig is by P. Barsch and Johann Balzer, from the Digital Library of Silesian Voivodeship. It is in the public domain because its copyright has expired.

41. The 1856 painting *The Blind Girl* by John Everett Millais is in the public domain because its copyright has expired. It is in the collection of the Birmingham Museum and Art Gallery, United Kingdom.

42. The 1910 woodblock print *Bat Before the Moon* by Biho Takashi is in the public domain because its copyright has expired. It is in the collection of the Brooklyn Museum.

43. The 1840 watercolor portrait of Ada Lovelace is by Alfred Edward Chalon. It is in the public domain because its copyright has expired.

44. The 1904 photograph of a boy wearing suspenders is from the Library of Congress, digital ID cph.3a00871. It is in the public domain because its copyright has expired.

45. The 1887 painting *October* by James Tissot is in the public domain because its copyright has expired. It is in the collection of the Montreal Museum of Arts.

46. The 1815 woodcut of a proposal is in the public domain because its copyright has expired.

47. The 2013 photograph of a Coober Pedy opal is copyright © D. Pulitzer, and is used here under CC BY-SA 3.0.

48. The 2011 photograph of a Cut Kiboko Gold tourmaline is copyright © Cowdisley, and is used here under CC BY-SA 3.0.

49. The 2009 photograph of an aquamarine was released into the public domain by its creator, Decym92.

50. The photograph of a coral necklace was provided to Wikimedia Commons by the National Museum of World Cultures, Tropenmuseum Collection, and is used here under CC BY-SA 3.0.
51. The painting *La Pia de' Tolomei* by Dante Gabriel Rossetti was painted between 1868 and 1880, and is in the public domain because its copyright has expired. It is in the Helen Foresman Spencer Museum of Art, Lawrence, Kansas.
52. The 1873 painting *Marigolds* by Dante Gabriel Rossetti is in the public domain because its copyright has expired. It is in the collection of the Castle Museum and Art Gallery, Nottingham.
53. The celestial sphere is from *Scenography of the Ptolemaic Cosmography*, by Johannes van Loon, based on Andreas Cellarius's *Harmonia Macrocosmica*, 1660. It is in the public domain because its copyright has expired.
54. The 17th century painting "Libra," from *The Signs of the Zodiac* by Jacob Jordaens, is in the Palais du Luxembourg, Paris. It is in the public domain because its copyright has expired.
55. The 1906 automobile calendar is by Edward Penfield, and is in the collection of the Library of Congress Prints and Photographs Division. It is in the public domain because its copyright has expired.
56. The 50-year perpetual calendar photograph is in the public domain.
57. The cartoon by John T. McCutcheon is from his 1905 collection *The Mysterious Stranger and Other Cartoons by John T. McCutcheon*. It is in the public domain because its copyright has expired.
58. The illustration "October" by Hans Thoma is from his late 19th century book *Festkalendar*. It is in the public domain because its copyright has expired.
59. The painting "October" is from the *Brevarium Grimani*, by Simon Bening, created circa 1510. It is in the public domain because its copyright has expired.

License Description and Terms

Aside from material purely in the public domain, photographs and other material in this book are used under specific licenses permitting free use, usually with an attribution requirement. For full text and terms of these licenses, click or enter the appropriate links below. If you believe there is an error in the copyright status or attribution of any of these images, please email us.

- Creative Commons Attribution 2.0 Generic (CC-BY 2.0): http://creativecommons.org/licenses/by/2.0/deed.en
- Creative Commons Attribution-Share Alike 3.0 Generic (CC-BY-SA 3.0): http://creativecommons.org/licenses/by-sa/3.0/
- Creative Commons Attribution-Share Alike 2.5 Generic (CC-BY-SA 2.5): http://creativecommons.org/licenses/by-sa/2.5/deed.en
- Creative Commons Attribution-Share Alike 2.0 Generic (CC-BY-SA 2.0): http://creativecommons.org/licenses/by/2.0/deed.en
- Creative Commons Attribution-Share Alike 1.0 Generic (CC-BY-SA 1.0): http://creativecommons.org/licenses/by-sa/1.0/deed.en
- CC0 1.0 Universal (CC0 1.0) Public Domain Dedication (CC0 1.0) http://creativecommons.org/publicdomain/zero/1.0/deed.en
- GNU Free Documentation License (GFDL): http://en.wikipedia.org/wiki/Wikipedia:Text_of_the_GNU_Free_Documentation_License
- License Art Libre (Free Art License): http://artlibre.org

October, Hans Thoma

Other Books from Timespinner Press

Timespinner
Press

The Story of a Special Day

Michael Dobson

A series of (eventually) 366 volumes covering everything that happened on your special day! Events, births, deaths, quotes, holidays, and much more. It's like a birthday card they'll never throw away!

US$7.95 print / US$2.99 ebook.

From Plassey to Pakistan

Humayun Mirza

The history of British Colonial India and the formation of Pakistan from the unique perspective of the son of Pakistan's first president and last of the royal line of Bengal, Bihar, and Orissa! This unique historical document tells the inside story of this distinguished family, including the detailed story of the coup that toppled his father from power!

US$27.95 print

A Whole New Navy: America's War in the Pacific

Miles Durr

The most comprehensive and detailed description of America's naval war in the Pacific ever—every battle, every ship, every task force and every task group from Pearl Harbor through the Japanese surrender! A must-have for the collection of every World War II buff!

US$29.95 print

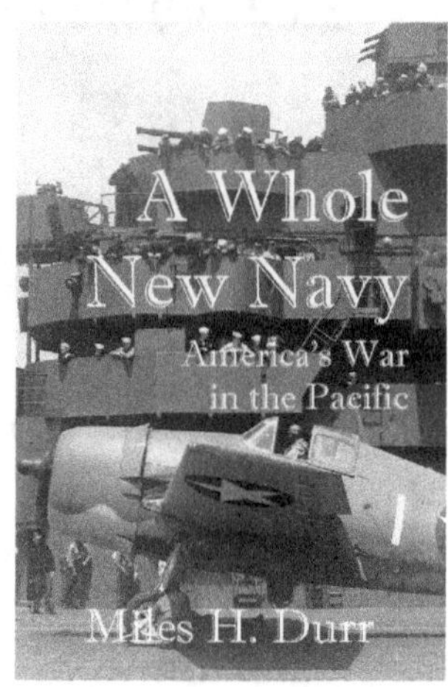

Improbable History: The Weird, the Obscure, and the Strangely Important

edited by Michael Dobson

From the birth of Western civilization to the rescue of Apollo 13, from the Leaning Tower of Pisa to Florence's Duomo, history has often turned on small, improbable details. Whatever happened to the ancient Samaritan people? Why did a fortuitous rainstorm allow the British to conquer India? How did an air raid in Italy lead to the development of chemotherapy? What happened when Albert Einstein met Adolf Hitler on the streets of Berlin? How did the Japanese manage to attack the US mainland using balloons? A cast of award-winning writers tackle some of the strangest tales in history!

US$19.95 print

The Letters of William Philip Schwartz 1842-1855

edited by John F. Schwartz

The 19th century soldier and adventurer William Philip Schwartz wrote a series of vivid and detailed letters chronicling his adventures in the Indian Wars, the Mexican-American War, the Gold Rush, and his term as Marine sergeant aboard the USS Constellation. A pioneer in photography, he took *the first known war photographs*. An unforgettable first-hand look into life in the 19th century!

US$17.95 print

Watergate Considered as an Organization Chart of Semi-Precious Stones (and other essays)

by Michael Dobson

In this light-hearted yet insightful tour through the Nixon White House, the Committee to Re-Elect the President, and the various investigative committees, you'll meet fascinating characters from Richard Nixon himself to such lieutenants as a G. Gordon Liddy and John Dean. You'll gain insights into the origin of the scandal, the motives of the players, and how the situation spiraled so badly out of control.

US$9.95 print/US$3.99 ebook

"October" from the *Brevarium Grimani* by Simon Bening (c.1510)

www.ingramcontent.com/pod-product-compliance
Lightning Source LLC
Chambersburg PA
CBHW060747260726
48660CB00002B/511